*To my Mom and my Aunt Jo-Anne,
thank you for sharing your love for costumes with me.*

Copyright © 2024 by Josée Lavoie

All rights reserved. The translation or reproduction of any excerpt of this book in any manner whatsoever, either electronically or mechanically and, more specifically, by photocopy and/or microfilm, is forbidden.

The Great Animal Costume Parade
© Text by Josée Lavoie. 2024
© Illustrations by Josée Lavoie. 2024

Published by Josée Lavoie

HeyJosee.com

ISBN: 978-1-990829-12-3

The Great Animal Costume Parade

Josée Lavoie

Leona loves to dress up in fun and colourful costumes.

She planned a big costume parade with all of her friends.

This year, they are all dressing up in animal costumes!

Leona is ready in her **leopard** costume.

Are you ready for The Great Animal Costume Parade?

Cameron is dressed up as a **chameleon**.

Deandra is dressed up as a deer.

Chad is dressed up as a **chicken**.

Skander is dressed up as a skunk.

Mouna is dressed up as a mouse.

Flavie is dressed up as a **flamingo**.

Lemi is dressed up as a **lemur**.

Freya is dressed up as a frog.

Shayan is dressed up as a **sheep**.

Paul is dressed up as a **panda**.

Elliot is dressed up as an **elephant**.

Octavia is dressed up as an **octopus**.

Jennifer is dressed up as a **jellyfish**.

Rachel is dressed up as a **raccoon**.

Bethany is dressed up as a **beaver**.

Finn is dressed up as a **fish**.

Dorothy is dressed up as a **dog**.

Craig is dressed up as a crab.

Petra is dressed up as a **peacock**.

Hiro is dressed up as a **hippopotamus.**

Scarlett is dressed up as a **squirrel**.

Cruz is dressed up as a **crocodile**.

Pia is dressed up as a **pig**.

Karim is dressed up as a **kangaroo**.

Gio is dressed up as a **giraffe**.

Henry is dressed up as a **hedgehog**.

Tulio is dressed up as a **turtle**.

Camila is dressed up as a **cat**.

Horatio is dressed up as a **horse**.

Timéa is dressed up as a **tiger**.

Ricardo is dressed up as a **rhinoceros**.

Zeynab is dressed up as a zebra.

Owen is dressed up as an **owl**.

Kora is dressed up as a **koala**.

Shayana is dressed up as a **shark**.

Fouad is dressed up as a **fox**.

Lambert is dressed up as a **llama**.

Lido is dressed up as a **lion**.

Rayna is dressed up as a **rabbit**.

Ben is dressed up as a **bear**.

Colette is dressed up as a cow.

Pablo is dressed up as a parrot.

Monica is dressed up as a monkey.

Percy is dressed up as a **penguin**.

The parade is done! Thank you for attending The Great Animal Costume Parade with Leona and her friends.

All of her friends had very nice costumes. Which costume is your favourite?

www.ingramcontent.com/pod-product-compliance
Lightning Source LLC
Chambersburg PA
CBHW042010150426
43195CB00002B/82